ABOUT YOUR AMBER

The gel that comes with this book looks a lot like amber. It is the sam[e]
Real amber, however, has hardened over millions of years. Before the ambe[r]
the gel, so sticky, in fact, that bugs could not crawl out of it.

Place your amber-encased bug on a windowsill so you can see light coming through it. You might want
to make a small display featuring your trapped bug. You can also play with the amber gel and with the plastic
bug inside. For example, you can mold the gel into a variety of shapes or make imprints of different objects in it.
Be sure to put the amber gel back in its jar and keep it covered when you're not using it, or it will dry up. Also, do
not let the gel freeze.

If you'd like, create your own amber-trapped "fossil," using the plastic bug that comes with this book. Or use
another small object. Cover the object with amber gel, flatten it with your hand, and leave it out to dry for a couple
of days. The gel will shrink a lot before it dries completely, so make sure you leave an
inch or two of amber gel around the edges of your "fossil."

WHAT IS AMBER?

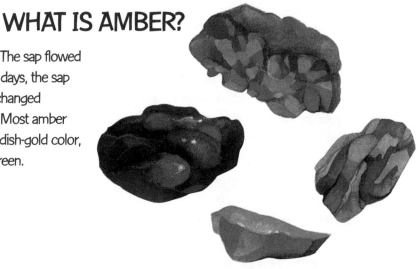

Amber is a fossilized resin, or sap. The sap flowed out of certain kinds of trees. After several days, the sap hardened. Then over millions of years, it changed chemically from a hard resin into amber. Most amber is easily recognized by its transparent, reddish-gold color, but some pieces of amber are blue and green.

Amber has been valued by people all over the world for thousands of years. Native Americans used amber in mixtures to help cure sickness and stop bleeding. Ancient Egyptians used amber to embalm their mummies. Amber has also been burned as incense to ward off evil spirits and mosquitoes.

Today, as in the past, amber is made into beautiful jewelry and art objects. Amber beads, earrings, and pendants, as well as carved amber chess sets, boxes, and mouthpieces for pipes, are on display in museums worldwide. Amber is also made into varnish, which is painted on the decks of ships and on finely crafted violins to keep their wood preserved.

INSECTS ARE SOME OF THE OLDEST LIVING ANIMALS

Spiders, scorpions, and the other creepy creatures mentioned in this book are all part of a family of animals called *arthropods*. All arthropods have skeletons or hard shells on the outside of their bodies. This "exoskeleton" protects the soft organs inside the body.

The first arthropods lived in the ocean, as did all life 400 to 500 million years ago. These arthropods were the ancestors of today's scorpions, spiders, and centipedes. Arthropods existed millions of years before people ever walked the earth. They are much older than even dinosaurs!

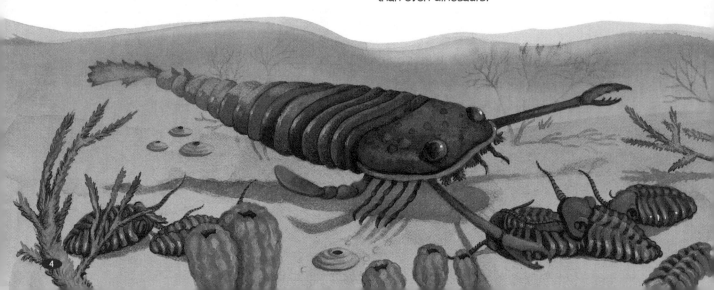

GIANT PREHISTORIC BUGS

While the first arthropods were swimming in the oceans, there was nothing growing on land. That's because most of the land was covered by water. Gradually, over millions of years, the land rose, some of the water dried up, and plants began to grow on land. The ancient ancestors of primitive creatures such as millipedes followed these plants out of the water.

Then, during the Carboniferous Period, 360–286 million years ago, more and more insects and other creepy creatures began to appear. The earth was covered with swamps, ferns, and damp soil—just the kind of place bugs like to live and grow. And grow they did! Giant dragonflies grew to have wingspans as wide as eighteen inches (46 cm)! Some scorpions were as long as a grown man is tall! Today giant scorpions and dragonflies no longer exist, but in those prehistoric times, few animals were larger than these bugs.

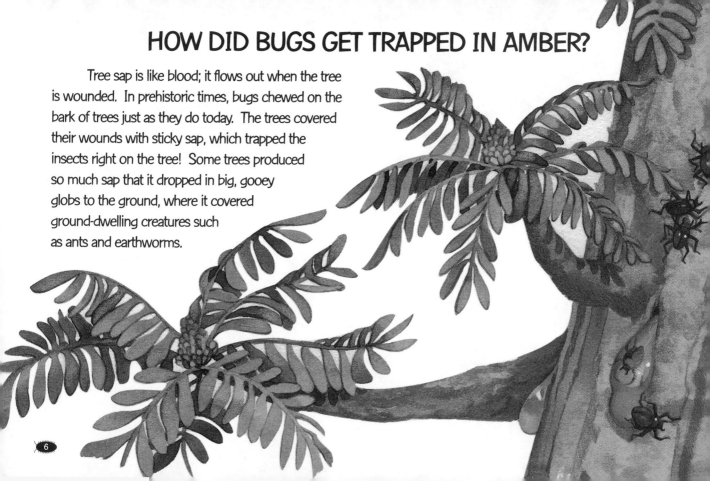

HOW DID BUGS GET TRAPPED IN AMBER?

Tree sap is like blood; it flows out when the tree is wounded. In prehistoric times, bugs chewed on the bark of trees just as they do today. The trees covered their wounds with sticky sap, which trapped the insects right on the tree! Some trees produced so much sap that it dropped in big, gooey globs to the ground, where it covered ground-dwelling creatures such as ants and earthworms.

After a while, the bugs caught in the tree sap died. Eventually, the sap was covered with mud from a flooded lake or river. Over millions of years, the mud surrounding the sap turned into clay or rock. Layers and more layers of mud and rock formed over the hard sap, and it gradually turned into amber.

Amber usually lies hidden deep inside the earth. People have found pieces of amber washed up on the shores of lakes and oceans in different places around the world. Amber is also mined on dry land in areas that once were covered with water. Compared to all the pieces of amber that have been found, the number that contain bugs or other evidence of prehistoric life is small.

WHAT KINDS OF BUGS WERE TRAPPED IN AMBER?

The earliest insects trapped in amber lived about 120 million years ago, during the Cretaceous Period. At that time, trees began to flower, and the earth's bug population expanded. But the bugs themselves didn't grow any bigger than the giant bugs of the Carboniferous Period.

How many different types of bugs can you name? The ancient ancestors of most of the bugs you can think of have been found trapped in amber.

Their size was what made the creepy creatures easy to trap. Only small arthropods got stuck in tree sap, because they were too small and weak to pull themselves out of the sticky resin.

AMBER DEPOSITS ARE FOUND ALL OVER

Most bugs live in warm, moist places. Scientists think that when the dinosaurs lived, the earth was warmer than it is today. So there were probably bugs everywhere!

Judging from the amber evidence, sap-producing trees grew in many parts of the world, particularly in the northern hemisphere. Bugs have been trapped in amber all over that area. Amber with trapped bugs has been

Ant: New Jersey

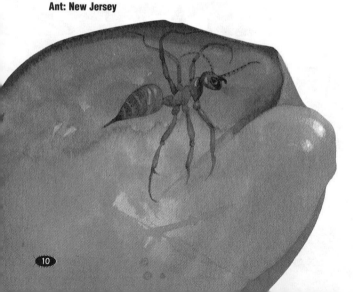

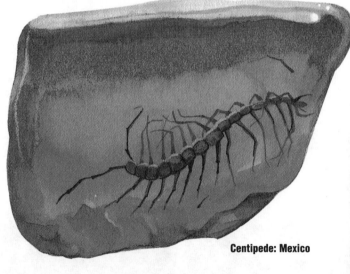

Centipede: Mexico

found in locations as diverse as Canada, Denmark, the Dominican Republic, Germany, Malaysia, Mexico, Poland, Russia, Sweden, and the United States.

Look closely at the bugs in the pictures below. Do they look like the bugs that you see today?

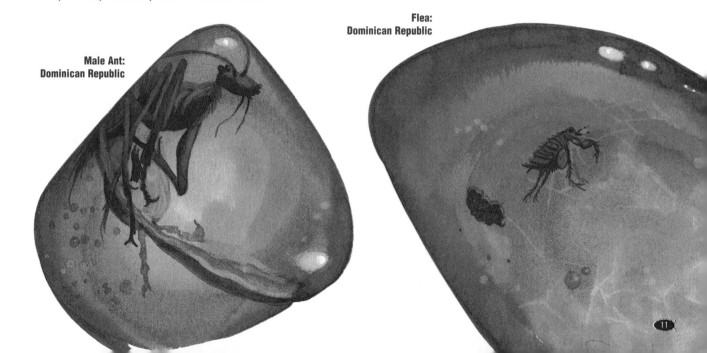

Male Ant:
Dominican Republic

Flea:
Dominican Republic

BUGS TODAY ARE A LOT LIKE PREHISTORIC BUGS

➡️ Because of amber's ability to preserve insects so well, scientists can closely compare ancient bugs to their descendants of today. Insects, like other animals, change and develop over the course of their lifespans. Pieces of amber containing ancient moths display the moths' three complete life stages before they become adults.

⬅️ Ancient scorpions and spiders shed their hard shells and grew new ones several times, just like these creatures do today. How do we know? The discarded shells were trapped in the amber, right next to the bugs. *Arachnids* (the scientific name for spiders and scorpions) have been trapped in their egg stage and as tiny babies just hatched. The babies look like the adults only smaller.

Many prehistoric insects ate the plants and flowers that grew in the ancient forests where they lived. Leaves, sticks, bark, and flowers have been found embedded in amber along with insects caught in the middle of their dinners.

Like their modern descendants, some prehistoric creepy creatures ate other bugs. Spiders and scorpions used their claws to hold their victims still, while their fangs or stingers shot poison into the other bug. Some spiders and scorpions were in the middle of devouring their prey when they were trapped in amber.

PREHISTORIC SNAPSHOTS

Scientists can tell a lot about how certain bugs lived by looking at what they were doing as they were frozen in time by amber. It is as if a picture had been taken of the past, when no humans were around to see for themselves. Here are some prehistoric snapshots:

➡ Some insects lived in colonies. This meant they lived together in groups and the old took care of the young. The stingless bee shown here was trapped in amber while carrying pollen on its hind legs. It was probably headed back to feed the other bees in the hive.

⬅ Some insects were vampires! Like their relatives today, ancient flies and mosquitoes sucked the blood of their victims. The mosquito shown here was trapped along with hairs from a mammal, most likely the source of its dinner. The bug's stomach was full, probably with blood!

Some arthropods liked to hitchhike. This group of baby scorpions was catching a ride on the mother scorpion's back when they were trapped in tree sap and preserved forever.

Some arachnids planned their meals. This spider was waiting to catch an unsuspecting bug in its sticky spider web when it was trapped in amber. Little did this spider know that instead of catching a bite to eat, it would be caught itself.

Some insects protected their young. These ants were caught in the act of taking young ants, or larvae, to safety. Perhaps they were being attacked by another ant colony or just fleeing from dripping resin.

CAN SCIENTISTS BRING PREHISTORIC CREATURES BACK TO LIFE?

Scientists today know how to extract cells and the stuff inside cells from ancient bugs trapped in amber. This includes a substance called DNA which is found in all living things. DNA is a molecule that acts as a code and determines many features of an organism.

Extracting DNA from ancient bugs is difficult and delicate work. The amber must be sliced very thinly and carefully so the inside of the bug can be opened up. Sometimes scientists find they are able to extract only fragments of ancient insect DNA. While scientists have learned a lot from studying this DNA, no one has ever brought an ancient bug back to life. At least not yet!

Could a dinosaur be brought back to life using blood from an amber-trapped mosquito? The answer is probably no. For one thing, scientists cannot get living cells to use ancient DNA, which is what they would need to do to grow a dinosaur.

Even if they cannot revive dinosaurs, scientists continue to study insects trapped in amber. As they unlock more of these creatures' secrets, scientists are better able to understand what the world was like millions and millions of years ago.